Teika Marija Smits

Russian Doll

Indigo Dreams Publishing

First Edition: Russian Doll
First published in Great Britain in 2021 by:
Indigo Dreams Publishing Ltd
24 Forest Houses
Halwill
Beaworthy
EX21 5UU
www.indigodreams.co.uk

Teika Marija Smits has asserted her right under the Copyright, Designs and Patents Act 1988 to be identified as the author of this work.

ISBN 978-1-912876-49-5

British Library Cataloguing in Publication Data. A CIP record for this book can be obtained from the British Library.

Designed and typeset in Palatino Linotype by Indigo Dreams.
Cover design from artwork by Jane Burn.
Printed and bound in Great Britain by 4edge Ltd.

Papers used by Indigo Dreams are recyclable products made from wood grown in sustainable forests following the guidance of the Forest Stewardship Council.

For Ludmila,
of course,
and
Rebecca and Jerome

CONTENTS

Daughter-doll
Doll-daughter

Mother-doll
Doll-mother

Daughter-doll
Doll-daughter

First Memories

Golden curtains
swaying in the breeze.

Sunlight, warmth,
the window beyond.

The rails of the cot,
an obstacle to my want.

Hypotheses, methods,
wriggling through my mind.

Limbs full of energy,
a talent for escape,

Mum and Dad asleep in bed,
surprised, though pleased, to see me.

Shades of Red

Once an actress, my Muscovite mother
knew how to make an entrance.
Striking in fuchsia
she'd arrive late
to my school performance,
call my name. Wave.
Have trouble finding her seat.

I'd glow crimson
and turn into the smallest
version of myself –
the littlest Russian doll,
the one most easily lost;
almost, but not quite,
invisible.

Mint Choc Chip

I
can still
remember
the excitement I
felt, thirty odd years ago,
when my sister announced
that the mint choc chip ice cream
she'd made was now ready to eat. It
was delicious, atop the bland shop-
bought cones that our mum had
somehow managed to get us.
xxxxxxxxxxxxxxxxxxxxxxxx
We ate every last bit of it,
savoured each sweet,
creamy mouthful,
and then I feasted
on the last of the
choc chips, the
survivors, still
clinging to
the plastic
tub. And
when it
was all
truly
gone,
how
sad
was
I

.

Anne Marie

Lugging my nine-year-old body
around the primary school track
as though it's a suitcase packed for every contingency –
from the sink of my belly
to the books in my head,
extra towels stored away in my throat and chest –
I force myself forwards,
through the traffic jam of summer air,
the blades of grass
sticky tarmac under my feet.

My best friend, quite unlike me, travels light.
A descendant of Atalanta,
she's inherited knowledge I'm not privy to:
the transmutation of cells
into slow-twitch muscle fibres
and an increased lung capacity;
the desire to be first,
the fastest on the field.

As she laps me with ease
I begin to comprehend
that just because I have the patience
of a tortoise
I won't always win.

Years later, once again,
I am conscious of the distance between us,
of secrets she'll never share,
as she makes a successful bid for heaven
by swallowing a bottle's worth of pills.

In the open coffin I am shown to
she is still.

There's no hint of a twitch
from those muscles
that could have outrun the world.

Ten Ton

My weight was 'ten ton',
according to the girl who was sleeping
in the bunk below me
during that Welsh residential
in which my belly strangely swelled
and I yearned for my teacher.

The end-of-trip disco was a disaster
(though I can't remember why)
and I fled to the dormitory,
only to be found by Paul Pateman,
who also had his share of fat-related nicknames.
I cried into his shoulder,
breathing in his musk
of boy-in-metamorphosis.

Later, when I discovered the streaks of red
that marked my shifting
from girl to woman
the nickname became a benediction –
a blessing of belonging from the group,
which was, I now knew,
as immutable
as I was changeable.

An Early Lesson in Fake News

One paper said that my mother, *The Venus of Vodka*,
was blonde;
another that *The Russian Doll*
was a sexy redhead.
A third was certain that the nude model,
From Russia With Love,
was brunette.

She planned world domination
by luring her art students – *lucky Eton boys* –
behind the Iron Curtain.

I was never mentioned,
except as a side note:
Mrs Smits lives in Windsor
with her husband and two daughters.
How fortunate for mousy-haired me.

Our Last Conversation

Driving home from Windsor in the dark,
traffic lights colourful with instructions,
my dad and I spoke of a film I'd just seen, *Inner Space*.

We wondered how quickly scientists would catch up
and make medics microscopic,
saving lives in miniature.

How was I to know that for my father,
they were already too late.

The Pulmonary Embolism

One day my father goes to the shops.
Walking back his lungs collapse, his legs give way,
he falls and *thud!* My world stops.

His heart rate soars (before it drops),
clouds roll in, the sky turns grey:
the day my father goes to the shops.

A passing neighbour, sees and stops,
he asks my dad if he's okay.
"I fell," he says. My world stops.

An ambulance comes, one more of the props
in this tragic, real life play;
performed the day my father goes to the shops.

The kindly paramedic mops
my father's brow. She knows she cannot say,
"It's just a fall." My world stops.

Now Death arrives to reap his crops,
and they all know today's the day,
the day he'll die, beside these shops;
he falls and *thud!* My world stops.

Mascara

As she prepares for the funeral,
carefully applying black gloop to her eyelashes,
she wonders if the prospect of black tear tracks –
ugly, stupid, childish –
on her powdered, made-up cheeks
is enough of a deterrent to weak, weak tears.

She is only fifteen and too young to understand
that water always finds a way to break through.

She stands in the hot, heaving church
and recites a poem to the mourners.

She wonders at the heat, the gall of the sun
to keep on shining.

She does not cry.

The tears come later, at night, in her room
when the mascara has already vanished.

Matryoshka

Death, now bored of its toy,
left the dolls in pieces, scattered,
some shut tight, permanently locked in grief,
others ripped apart, heads rolling
at their feet.

The littlest doll found herself rattling around
in the wrong size body,
suddenly bulky with responsibilities
and listening to echoes.
To all eyes an adult, within, a child.

The Colour of a Conference Pear

She chooses three conference pears
as the subjects of her still life
because they remind her of her father.

When she was a girl, come autumn
the fruit bowl bore only one fruit:
the conference pear.

They came from the tree
at the end of their garden;
the one not good enough for climbing.

Her father would crunch
his way through the bowl, saying,
"We need to eat these up."

Yet she had no taste for them.
The flesh was too hard, the skin too bitter,
its texture too rough, its green too brown.

It was only decades later that she discovered
that they soften up beautifully when cooked.
A dessert pear, they are meant for desserts.

As she begins to sketch the pears
she has a longing for the impossible –
to bake him her now-favourite pudding: pear crumble.

Later, she chooses her colours,
considers the greens and yellows and browns
she will use in her painting.

With older eyes she sees the colours better;
the brown is not brown but green-gold,
the green is not green but yellow with a touch of emerald.

The colours complement each other,
they are warm, unshowy, and subtle in their beauty.
She can see this now.

Mother-doll
Doll-mother

Making Heartroom

Inspired by *How Mothers Love* by Naomi Stadlen

This mother's womb grows day by day,
but so too does her heart.
She homes the house guest come to stay
within her womb, which grows each day;
and though her child will soon away
there'll be no sorrow when they part.
This mother's womb grows day by day,
but so too does her heart.

Treasure

Curiosity, and a sudden thirst for savagery,
makes her split open the matryoshka –
pop pop pop pop pop –
until *ah!*
how satisfying,
the baby doll rests snug in her palms.

Changeling

By the time you'd conjured yourself up
out of nothing more than love and cells,
I knew too much about changelings,
the wickedness of fairies.

So when you made me sick and round and fat,
unable to think or feel or care,
I couldn't help but wonder
if I'd already been tricked.

Fairies are not to be underestimated.

And when, after nine months, you demanded
to be let out, to be with your fairy kin
I couldn't help but scream:
"Go, go, go!"

Your father, understanding my fear,
gently placed you on my chest,
reminded me of our protections:
the iron tablets I'd been taking, the boxwood round the house,
and allowed me to fall in love with you.

Shadows and Bones

My long-dead ancestor, her bones now bleached and washed
and hung out to dry,
suckles her child as she strives
to make sense of the shadows in the cave.

She knows that the fire,
bringing warmth to her long-dead bones,
is a living thing, although it is easily killed.
It licks the cave with its dry, sparking tongue.

Yet what are the shadows? Alive or dead?
They rattle her bones – these strange, swaying folk,
who surround the fire and dance
in the walls of the cave.

She is weary to the bone, so she closes her eyes
but the shadows remain, to flicker and dance
in the black of her cave mind.
Her child suckles and sleeps, and so does she

and she dreams of shadows and shifting shapes and heat.

Hooke's Law

A scientific law in which the force necessary to extend or compress
a spring by a certain distance scales in a linear fashion with respect to
that distance.

The mothers of two or more
said there'd be love enough
to go around.
Plenty.
That my heart would stretch
and flex like a spring.

Still

looking beyond my mushrooming belly,
to where my heart's joy, my firstborn, sat playing,
I wasn't convinced.

Yet when my son was born
I discovered they were right
and Hooke was wrong.
We mothers have hearts that do not obey
the laws of physics;
we have no elastic limits.

The Swimming Lesson

We take it in turns to show interest
in the swimming lesson,
to wave at our children
when they pause,
panting from their exertions,
to seek our approval.
We direct remarks at each other:
"Isn't it hot?"
"They need to get some air in here."

I watch my daughter,
part mermaid, part astronaut,
glide and then kick
her way through the water;
and I long to join her –
to escape the heat,
the small talk and screens,
the gravity that binds me
to this sticky plastic seat.

The Right Tool

Unlike his Russian grandmother,
who has a tendency to use the one tool –
a knife –
for everything from sawing and scraping
to peeling and digging,
my son understands the importance
of using the right tool for the job.

As I walk around his new Minecraft world,
strangely blocky in my Alex skin,
he patiently reminds me that an axe
is best for chopping trees,
a shovel for digging dirt and sand and gravel,
a pickaxe for mining stone,
a hoe for tilling soil.

At nightfall, when the zombies come groaning,
he instructs me to wield a sword.
Terrified by these computer-generated monsters,
I scream and run,
suddenly nostalgic
for the safe simplicity of Tetris.

Mouthguard

Every night while she sleeps
the story that she dare not tell
gnaws its way out of her mouth,
pounding at her jaws to be let out
until
another fractured molar
sends her to the dentist
who talks of 'bruxism', teeth grinding, jaw clenching
and, with all the godmotherly concern she can muster,
asks her if she's suffering from stress.

The story titters,
makes her angry, deceitful.
"No, everything's fine."
The dentist says nothing
so she fills the silence with, "You know,
the usual... work, money, family."

The dentist nods
and casts a spell of protection over the woman,
gagging the story
with a curious-looking sentinel
that fits her hapless mouth perfectly.

Russian Doll

I am heavy with the hopes
of my younger selves – the ones
who dreamt of all I could be.

They call to me, disappointed,
as my once-bright dress
begins to dull, as I thin

and am worn smooth by little hands
that dismantle me daily.
I answer with excuses and apologies.

Life intrudes, I explain;
takes us apart
and rebuilds us askew.

The Swing

With aching limbs and clicking joints
I climb onto the swing.
I push the air with straightened legs,
and quickly gather speed.

A pendulum of sorts am I –
with limbs that ache no more.
The years recede as I gain height;
I'm borne, reborn, in air.

Now childhood dreams of long ago –
heady, poignant, sweet –
rush within, stir memories,
ignite a sleeping flame.

A smile unbidden, curves my lips
as I recall the days
of playground games and wobbly teeth,
the smell of just-cut grass.

My cares recede; I'm old no more
and all there is, is this:
the back and forth, the up and down.
The sun, the sky, the swing.

Acknowledgements

With many thanks to the editors of the following magazines/publications in which these poems were previously published:

'Shades of Red' first appeared in *Prole*, Issue 27. 'Mint Choc Chip' was first published in *Food and Drink: Bramley Apple Festival Poems, 2015*. 'An Early Lesson in Fake News' was first published in *Ink, Sweat and Tears*. 'The Pulmonary Embolism' was first published in *LossLit*, Issue 5. 'The Colour of a Conference Pear' first appeared in *The Lake*. 'Making Heartroom' first appeared in the *Bonnie's Crew* anthology and 'The Swimming Lesson' first appeared in *Brittle Star*, Issue 39. 'Russian Doll' was first published in *Atrium* and 'The Swing' took second place in the Swanezine poetry competition 2013.

I am grateful to Helena Nelson for her kind and constructive critiques of some of these poems. Thanks also go to my husband, Tom, a non-poetry reader who would occasionally say "I liked that one!" when listening to me read some of these poems. Those words made me happier than you can imagine. Finally, I give thanks to God for planting within me the storytelling seed, and, of course, for everything else.

Russian Doll is Teika's debut collection.

Indigo Dreams Publishing Ltd
24, Forest Houses
Cookworthy Moor
Halwill
Beaworthy
Devon
EX21 5UU
www.indigodreams.co.uk